A PLACE IN THE STAFF

Jen Rafferty

A PLACE IN THE STAFF
Finding Your Way as a Music Teacher

Jen Rafferty

A Place in the Staff:
Finding Your Way as a Music Teacher

Copyright © 2019 Jen Rafferty

Cover design by Molly Andrejko
Interior layout by Hopko Designs
Author photograph by Chelsea Fausel

First Edition

ISBN: 0-578-59484-6
ISBN-13: 978-0-578-59484-2

TABLE OF CONTENTS

"A teacher affects eternity; he can never tell where his influence stops." ~ *Henry Adams*

INTRODUCTION

Congratulations on your teaching job! As you begin this incredible adventure, I want you to understand something: teachers are superheroes. Seriously. You are a superhero! Your power allows you to teach a child and potentially affect the course of history! How amazing is that? You get to cultivate a generation of thinkers, foster curiosity, and, of course, help your students discover the music within each of them.

You are not in this alone. You are joining forces alongside educators who are passionate, smart, and fierce advocates for their students. As a music teacher you have a tremendous opportunity to influence an entire community. You will empower your students to understand that their voices can make a difference, and teach them how to express themselves through this fine art. You have the superpower to literally change lives.

And now, you're finally in your classroom! So just in case you didn't know, in addition to your superhero status, there are many other roles that you will have to fill. You will soon find that although you will be teaching music, you will also be responsible for instructing your students about behavior, perseverance, organization, manners, leadership, self-regulation, time management, social skills, and sometimes hygiene. If you weren't aware yet, in the very small print of your contract, the job description also included event planner, grant writer, director, advocate, repair person, counselor, multitasker, travel agent, role model, fundraiser, negotiator, and copy machine technician. The good news is that there is a large community of teachers, and we're all in this together.

This book is not about music pedagogy. It's also not about standards or curriculum. In these pages you will discover all the things in between the lines. It's about the stuff that happens in your first few years of teaching that nobody told you about when you were in college. To be completely honest, I almost left the teaching profession after my first year. No one prepared me for the amount of emotional, psychological, and physical stress that is common amongst first year teachers. I thought something was wrong with me. I started to question my abilities as a teacher (and all of my life choices that led me to this career)! I felt this way despite knowing deep down that teaching was really the only thing I ever wanted to do. I don't know what I would have done if I made the decision to leave. And fortunately, I didn't. So I wrote this book for you who might also feel completely overwhelmed and lost at the beginning of your career.

This book will guide you in understanding your students and school culture, give you important ideas for music advocacy, provide resources for getting instruments and equipment, and remind you to take care of yourself, especially when things are difficult. Use the spaces provided to reflect, plan, and capture moments of inspiration. As you go through the school year, these notes will become a helpful tool for you.

Your first years as a teacher can be both exciting and extremely overwhelming. It's okay to cry. And you might cry a lot! No one told me that. So I am telling you this again: it's okay to cry! Teaching music is important work — superhero work! I'm sure you care a great deal about the success of your students and making a positive impact on their lives. But please keep this in mind: you might see kids come through your door whose home lives are tragically impossible to imagine. You will have lessons that will completely fail. You will have to deal with state tests and assemblies that take time away from you and your students. You will have concerts where the students are not as prepared as you had hoped, or some may not bother to show up at all.

Though you will undoubtedly need to navigate through challenges, you will also come to know incredible moments of joy, laughter, and beautiful music-making. You can be a beacon of inspiration and comfort for many kids. You will have the chance to rework a failed lesson because you'll learn from your mistakes and can anticipate where the challenges will be. You will learn to be flexible and advocate for the needs of all your students. You will understand the difference between performance and process, and will hopefully honor them both. And, you will learn how to be a dependable colleague, a seasoned teacher, and a trusted adult for the students who value your guidance.

Teaching truly lays the foundation for every other career. We provide the building blocks for our students' futures. In your music classroom, you have the power to inspire students to love school and pave the way for lifelong learning… and once in a while, fix the paper jam in the copy machine.

1.
REMEMBER YOUR WHY

"Education in music is most sovereign because more than anything else, rhythm and harmony find their way to the innermost soul and take strongest hold upon it." ~ Plato

Most likely, you didn't become a teacher by chance. You've spent a ton of time in school and worked hard to get into your own classroom. Your passion and commitment to this profession can probably be traced back to a significant moment (or moments) in your life.

For me, teaching music was a calling. I just seemed to know that it was what I was supposed to do. When I was twenty-seven, my mother moved out of my childhood home, and during my last visit to the house, I spent a good part of an afternoon cleaning out my old room. In one of the drawers I found my middle school choir portfolio that I had saved. I remember my twelve-year-old self thinking that I should keep it just in case I needed it when I had my own classroom someday. Yes, I am aware that this is super nerdy, but there were actually some useful things in there! Way to go, younger Jen!

What really sealed the deal for me was my high school choir director, Eric Williams. Mr. Williams lived and breathed music, and was insistent that each of his students become the best version of him or herself. He pushed us each day to make music with every molecule of our being. He would often remind us that music is an innate gift that we must cherish and nurture. It gives us the ability to evoke emotion in another human being. Mr. Williams told me that people never actually create music. The music was already there inside of me. It's inside of everyone. We just have to discover a way to let it out. As my music teacher, his job was to help me find it. I knew that was my calling too.

Take a minute and think about your inspiration to become a music teacher. What is your story? Who or what led you to this path? Describe it here with as much detail as you can remember:

_____

_____

_____

_____

_____

With that memory fresh in your mind, describe why you wanted to teach music:

The words above are what I will refer to throughout the book as your *why.* Your *why* is incredibly powerful because it will give you roots to ground you in situations when you feel unsure of yourself. It can change a frustrating situation into something that will challenge you to grow. A difficult interaction with a student can transform into an opportunity for reflection. Your *why* should serve as the foundation for everything you do. This includes your philosophy about your music program, the way you assess your students, and how often you communicate with parents.

Read through your story and your *why* that you wrote in the previous section. If it isn't already, play with the wording so it is only one or two sentences. This shortened version will serve as a quick reminder for you so it is easy to remember.

_____

_____

_____

_____

_____

Keep this *why* close to you so you can recall it easily. It can be helpful to write it on a piece of paper and put it in your desk. This constant reminder will serve you well when you have decisions to make or if you need to advocate for something.

Here's my *why*:
I teach music to help people discover the music that exists inside of them.

This is my professional mission. This helps me focus on things that are most important to me. It has become my anchor when I feel lost. If I am unsure of something, I go back to my *why* so I can make a decision with confidence.

SETTING PROFESSIONAL GOALS

Now that your *why* is established and easy to recall, the next step is to determine where you are going and how you'll get there. These are your professional goals: your destination. Where do you see yourself in one year? Three years? Five? What do you want to accomplish?

This is an exercise I do at the beginning of every

school year. Goal-setting is a great way to focus your efforts on a few things that are really important, instead of thinking that everything is of equal importance. Everything cannot have equal importance. I have seen many new teachers dive into everything with all of their energy, and this has always led quickly to burnout. Goal-setting and remembering your *why* will steer you in a very specific direction.

Since my *why* is "to help people discover the music that exists inside of them," one of my yearly goals is to make at least two community connections throughout the school year by taking students out to perform, or inviting community members into the classroom. Content-based goals are necessary too, but for this exercise, content and standards-based goals should be woven within the larger professional ones.

Your goals should be **S**pecific, **M**easurable, **A**ttainable, **R**elevant, and **T**ime-based (**SMART**). Here is my goal as an example for the acronym:

SMART goal:
Make at least two community connections throughout the year by either taking my students out to perform, or inviting community members into our classroom.

Specific
The community connection will be out in the greater community or I will invite community members into the classroom.

Measureable
Two throughout the year.

Attainable
I might need to find community events where we can participate. I'll also need to work out a few details like transportation and permission slips.

Relevant
Community connections are relevant to my students and my district philosophy.

Time-based
I will complete this goal by the end of the school year.

SMART goals set you up for greater achievement by laying the groundwork for success. On the other hand, if my goal was "to have my students discover their sound," this would not be something on which I could focus my efforts or bring to an administrator. She'd probably say, "Well, that sounds lovely, Jen, but what does that mean?" Here's why:

Specific
What does "discover their sound" look or sound like?

Measureable
How would I determine if a sound was discovered?

Attainable
How would I go about reaching this goal?

Relevant
You can probably argue that this goal is relevant.

Time-based
There is no timeline attached to this goal.

To create your **SMART** goals, you have to decide what is important to you as a music teacher. What do you need to do in order to achieve your *why*? Use the space below to brainstorm things that you want to accomplish this year at school:

_____

_____

_____

_____

_____

Take a look at your list. Are your goals specific? Measurable? Attainable? Relevant? Time-based? Goal-setting is only effective if you have a way to measure whether or not you met it.

Now, choose three of the goals that you listed above. What do you need to make them happen? Think about resources, time, and materials. Perhaps you need to reorganize the classroom or rehearsal space. It might require a decision about the use of certain assessments, or the type of music you will have the students play or sing.

To be clear, if you don't meet your goal, it doesn't mean that your efforts were a complete failure. Goal-setting and reassessing those goals should be an ongoing process. These are *your* professional goals that can be tweaked and changed at any time. Reflect and assess why it didn't work out, and put it back through the **SMART** model. Was it a realistic goal for your teaching situation? Were your expectations reasonable? Did you have all of the resources to make it happen? Adjust the goal as needed to set you and your students up for success.

It's important to remember that failure is part of learning. We tell this to our students all the time, right? Trust the process and embrace the missteps because that is where the learning happens. Your goals will shift and change. Perhaps you started off with one idea, and then something else came along that inspired you to take a new direction towards fulfilling your *why*. Whatever your goals may be, they will give you a clear objective and help you determine where you want to invest your energy and how you want to spend your time.

2.
FINDING YOUR PLACE

"The greatness of a community is most accurately measured by the compassionate actions of its members." ~ Coretta Scott King

School culture may not always be tangible, but it can be incredibly obvious. You can get a feel for the way of life at a school from the moment you step inside. There is evidence of the culture from what is posted on the walls, in the attitude of the teachers, and the conversations of the students in the hallway. As a new addition to the school, you are most likely entering an already established community. You need to figure out your place and enhance the school culture as the music teacher.

You probably have plenty of ideas for lessons, interesting projects and repertoire for your classes, and it can be easy to get caught up in what you have to bring to the table. It is equally important to remember that you are a part of a much bigger team. Most of the people working at your school have likely been there for a long time and have helped build the existing traditions and culture.

You have to find a way to get a pulse on how the school operates. Often this just means you need to pay attention to the students and staff. Listen to the chatter as you pass through the halls, the tone of the faculty meetings, and notice the dynamics between teachers and parents. Understanding school culture is one of those ambiguous aspects of teaching that can't necessarily be taught, yet it is essential to feeling like you fit in with your school community. You have a point of view and a job to do, but be mindful that you are a piece of a much larger puzzle. To do your job well, you have to figure out what the rest of the puzzle looks like!

Learn about the values of your school. What is the mission or school motto? How does the school honor its mission? What does the school community celebrate? Once you have some of these answers, start to ask yourself how you can use your music program to elevate or add to what already exists.

For example, at my first teaching job, the school had a tradition of frequently celebrating athletic accomplishments. Every Monday, the morning announcements included "This Week in Sports." We heard about the upcoming games, last week's scores, or a short bio highlighting an exemplary student athlete. Listening to how the school recognized students in this way, I proposed adding "This Week in Music" to ensure the music students had their moment alongside the athletes. It made the music program more visible and kept everyone informed about the musical events happening throughout the year. It was also pretty cool when the athlete of the week was recognized for his or her musical achievements as well.

FIND YOUR TRIBE

Music teachers can sometimes feel isolated. You might be the only music teacher in your building (or you are always busy in your classroom teaching lessons). It's extremely important to get to know the other teachers in your school. They can be great allies. Seek out collaborative opportunities as a way to work with them and learn about other subject areas. Eating lunch somewhere other than your desk might be a good place to start.

The faculty room can sometimes be a friendly place, but it might actually be a spot that you want to avoid. When I was a new teacher, I did not like spending time in the faculty room. Instead of a restorative 30 minutes, I always got an earful of complaints from grumpy teachers. If there is negative rhetoric in the faculty lounge, get out quickly and eat lunch somewhere else. Negativity is contagious and unhelpful. Unfortunately, there will always be some negativity shared by a few people in any workplace. To be clear, venting is not the same as being negative. Venting (to a safe person) is okay and very important sometimes! But the naysayers and downers are always looking for fresh faces with whom they can wallow in their woes. Don't fall in the trap. Listen if you must, then politely excuse yourself.

As an alternative, seek out the most passionate and positive teachers in your building and talk with them. Find the teachers whose *why* aligns with yours. These are the people who will keep the enthusiasm and momentum going even when things get tough. They usually have a great vision for their school and are always looking to try new things. Make connections with them and explore ways to work together. Spend some time picking their brains and exchange ideas about education.

Be sure to ask other people for guidance and advice. Talk with the should-have-been-retired-six-years-ago teacher who wears the comfy loafers. She knows what she's talking about; definitely ask her! She probably has an interesting perspective on any questions you might have. Seek out opportunities to observe other teachers. This is a practice that usually stops once you are out of college, but is one of the best ways to learn while getting to know other teachers in your building. If you can't get out of your classroom to observe another music teacher, ask your principal if you can observe an English or science class. It's good to see how other teachers handle different situations so you will be able to add to your toolbox of teaching techniques.

Although the principal's name might be on the letterhead, it's no secret that the custodians and secretaries run every school. These people will be your best friends. They have an important viewpoint on how the school is run, and they are also the keepers of the keys to get anywhere in the building! They will help you set up risers, get extra pencils from the supply closet, and open a locked room. Be especially gracious to these people. Their jobs are often overlooked because they stay in the background, making sure things run smoothly. Be kind and thank them often.

Here is an example of a **SMART** goal that can help you connect with other teachers. Use mine or create your own:

This school year I will reach out to three teachers outside of my department to check in about shared students. I'll ask them about what they do in the classroom, and I will share some things that I am trying in my class.

Specific
I will ask about shared students and exchange ideas.

Measurable
I will talk with three teachers.

Attainable
I work with 30 other teachers in my building, so talking with three of them is reasonable.

Relevant
I will learn about different teaching techniques which will ultimately make me a better teacher and feel more connected to my school community.

Time-based
I will complete this goal within this school year.

Your **SMART** goal:_____

_____

_____

_____

_____

ALL IN THIS TOGETHER

Once you develop relationships with classroom teachers, it is much easier to ask for help or guidance. This relationship can be especially important if you pull students out for lessons. Every teacher should be on the same team supporting students. The switch from "my students" to "our students" is sometimes difficult for teachers to understand, particularly when dealing with missed class time for lessons or other music events. When a teacher comes to you to discuss a student missing his or her class, the words "my student" and "my time" usually make their way into the conversation. It is really important to use phrases like "our students" and "the student's time." This small change in language can have a really positive result by putting everyone on the same side in supporting the needs of all our students, especially if they are a part of the music program. This also means that it is your responsibility to work with the classroom teachers and listen to their concerns. If we are all in fact working towards the success of our students, you must be flexible as well. Again, building relationships is absolutely necessary.

The more you can involve other people in your class, the more they will feel connected to what you are doing. I often have visitors come into my room, particularly during my guitar unit. One time an administrator, Mr. Zarcone, came to do his mandatory observation. After class he commented on how he was never able to play guitar. He complained that his fingers were too fat, and didn't move fast enough. While I could have smiled and nodded, instead, I said, "I have at least two kids in each of my classes with that same attitude, and they learn it anyway!" He looked at me for a second, unsure as to what to say. He seemed surprised by his own excuses and decided that he would learn to play the guitar. After that day, Mr. Zarcone frequently stopped by to practice and even played with the kids at the concert.

It may feel intimidating to have other teachers and administrators in your classroom, but an open door policy can have a huge impact on your program. By participating in my class, Mr. Zarcone was able gain new insight, appreciation, and understanding of what my students experienced. And as a bonus, he learned a new skill and discovered that he could move his fingers just fine.

It is crucial for other teachers to see what happens in music class so they understand that the kids participate in a different way than they do in other disciplines. It's not uncommon for particular students who are troublesome in a math class to be thriving in music class. As I mentioned before, it's necessary to see how you fit into the larger picture. It is equally important that the other teachers know what your piece of the puzzle looks like, too. They may be inspired by your teaching techniques and find new ways to engage students during their lessons. Give them a chance to do that!

GET INVOLVED

Find ways to be involved with extracurricular activities outside of music. Help out with an after school club or learn something new along with the students. To be clear, I am not suggesting you do everything. You can't do everything, and it's important to figure out your boundaries (more about that in a later chapter). However, if time allows, it can be really nice for you and the students to interact outside of the music classroom.

A few years ago, I discovered that one of my students was interested in coding and went to Coding Club every Wednesday in the math room. I had never coded anything before, and it always seemed very intimidating, but I thought this might be a low pressure opportunity to give it a try. I stopped in on a Wednesday after school and signed up for the computer programming website they were using. It was actually pretty cool! I made a stronger connection with my student and got to know the math teacher a little bit. He was surprised by my interest, and was really happy to help, (and I definitely needed it). Don't be afraid to try something new.

The more involved you are, the more students and other teachers will start to see you as a well-rounded person instead of a one-dimensional music teacher. Chaperone a school dance, go to a basketball game, or sit in on the book presentation in ELA class. Again, teaching is all about building relationships. If you really know your students, you will be able to teach them better, and they will be more likely to want to learn from you.

School culture is something you will help create now that you are a part of the staff! Remember, when you take a litmus test on culture, if you look for the negative and irritating things that happen at school, I guarantee that you will find them. However, if you look for the fun, enthusiasm, and joy in your building, I promise you will find that, too. You will always find what you look for.

3.
THE PARENT CONNECTION

Stay committed to your decisions; but stay flexible in your approach. ~ Tony Robbins

The parents of your students can be an important lifeline. They will be some of your biggest allies and a tremendous help when you need it. These connections bridge the gap between home and school as students start to see that we are all advocating for their success. All teachers must foster positive relationships with parents, but it's especially important for music teachers. Parents have the potential to be great partners and fierce supporters of your program.

It can be very meaningful to share something positive with parents right from the beginning of the year. Let them know about what's happening in your classroom or during your rehearsals. Electronic newsletters provide a great opportunity to add a link to a video of a lesson so parents can actually see what is happening in school. Consider sharing songs that you are playing or learning about in class. If a newsletter doesn't exist, create your own.

Another great way to reach out to parents is to send home a "Good News" card. This can simply be a postcard with a short note saying something positive that a student did in class. Everyone loves getting mail, and this card can be something that is proudly displayed on the refrigerator at home. I once sent a "Good News" card home to a high school student that really struggled in other classes. His parents were thrilled with my note, especially since they were usually overwhelmed with negative communication regarding their son. Because I learned that they were not getting much positive feedback from the school, I frequently let them know when he did well in my classroom.

It's always good practice to do even small check-ins with parents. This opens the door for future conversations. It can be as simple as "Allie had a fantastic clarinet lesson today. Just wanted to let you know!" Though it may be tempting to send this kind of communication by email, a phone call can sometimes be better. When we speak on the phone, it allows for immediate dialogue that can lead to a deeper understanding of the student. If talking on the phone is not your strong suit, practice with a colleague. Depending on the reason for the correspondence, an email might suffice, but first consider reaching out by phone.

To further connect with parents, find out about your school's Parent Teacher Association or Music Boosters organization. If parent groups are not yet established, perhaps there are some enthusiastic parents who could start one. These parents can help support events, organize a fundraiser, or hand out snacks on a field trip. When the parents are involved, they will feel connected with you and your work with their kids. Also, when students see their parents involved, they too become more invested in their own learning at school.

COMMUNICATING WHEN THINGS AREN'T SO GREAT

Sometimes you may have to reach out to a parent because of something that isn't going well in class. As a newer teacher, talking to parents about these situations can feel intimidating. Hopefully you have already started a line of communication earlier in the year, so this won't be the first time calling home. Keep it simple and stick to the facts. It can be easy to input subjective commentary, however, try to be as objective as possible. What did the student do? What did you do to help the situation?

When you begin the conversation, start with something positive if you can. This will help paint a well-rounded picture of what is happening and acknowledges that there are some things that are going well in class. Let the parents know what you have done to help and then ask for their support. Explain that together you are a team in guiding their child toward academic improvement. Here is an example:

> Hi, Mrs. Smith. This is Mrs. Rafferty, Hannah's music teacher. I just wanted to touch base with you about some things going on in class. First of all, Hannah has great energy and has a lot of potential to be a leader. Recently, however, she has been talking with her neighbors when she should be participating in class activities. This distracts the other students and ends up disrupting class. I know she has the ability to do well. I have reminded her of the class

expectations many times. I moved her seat to a place where we thought would work better, but it hasn't seemed to help. I told her I would be contacting you so we could all be on the same page in helping Hannah be successful. Is there any way you can help by speaking with her about her behavior in class?

If the situation calls for it, having a meeting in person is best. The guidance counselors can usually help set this up. I remember my first meeting with an irate parent, trying to explain that her child's behavior in my class was becoming disruptive. I was very nervous walking into the meeting, but I made sure that I had the support of the guidance counselors and the principal so they could help me navigate the interaction. After the meeting I breathed a sigh of relief, but I remember thinking to myself, "Who am I, a brand new teacher, to tell this parent about her child's behavior? What do I know?" I felt insecure about my words when talking about behavior problems in the classroom. I often considered that it was easier to let bad behavior go than to speak to a parent. However, when I remembered my *why*, I understood that parent communication was an essential piece to help students with their undesirable behaviors.

As a parent of two children myself, I appreciate any feedback that I get about how they are doing in school. I want my kids to know that I have a stake in their education. They know my husband and I are on the same team as their teacher, guiding them to be their best selves, both academically and socially. More often than not, parents are grateful for your communication. It's much better to be proactive and reach out earlier than let them wait to see the comments on their child's report card.

If you establish personal contact with parents

early in the year, then you are able to further build upon that relationship. During the first two months of school, write an email, call, or send a note home praising their child for something they did well. Later on, if you have to reach out for something negative, it won't be the first time they have heard from you. The small gesture can bring huge smiles to a family, and begin an important dialogue between you and parents.

There will be occasions when you reach out to a student's parents and they are not in the picture or not receptive to your attempts to communicate. Some family situations will break your heart. There may be times when parents don't (or won't) want to be a part of their child's education. Sometimes they don't know how. Sometimes parents themselves had a hard time in school as a student and don't value education. Unfortunately, this sentiment can be passed on to their children. You need to try to connect with these parents too. We may not change their point of view, but you can hopefully start a conversation that could be productive and helpful for the student.

Carve out time weekly to send a message to a few parents. Even just a handful of home contacts each week can make a huge difference in your program. It's a good idea to maintain a record by keeping a class list on hand. Put a check mark next to the student's name and add a small note about when you contacted someone at home, and what you spoke about. Think about how communicating with parents can bring you closer to your *why*. When the students know that you and their parents are on the same side, it can completely change the way they experience school. You will also feel more strongly connected with your students and school community.

Here is an example of a **SMART** goal about parent communication. Use mine or create your own.

This school year I will communicate with parents at least four times each week.

Your **SMART** goal:_____

_____

_____

_____

4.
KNOW YOUR STUDENTS
(AKA CLASSROOM MANAGEMENT)

*"Correction does much, but encouragement
does more." ~ Goethe*

When I first started teaching 7th grade general music, I really struggled with classroom management. My class sizes were large and the space was always too small. I felt that no matter what I did, some of the kids would hijack the room and ruin it for everyone else. Each year there seemed to be one class that gave me the most grief because of a few students. I would sigh in relief when I found out that one of my students wasn't in school on his general music days because I knew the class would run more smoothly. Sometimes I lost sleep the night before one of my behavior-challenged classes.

In the beginning I tried incentives like chocolates, point charts, and even rewards of ice cream parties for good behavior. I went to a few workshops and read lots of books about classroom management and motivation. I understood that it was necessary to build relationships with each student in order to help with classroom management, but, to be honest, it's hard to have a good relationship with every single student. There are some students that struggle with any type of connection, and it's difficult to want to make a connection with a student who consistently disrupts class. I knew I needed to teach everybody. My *why* included everybody! But it was clear that my classroom "management" was not working. I couldn't seem to figure out what I was doing wrong.

Eventually, I started to notice that the behavior of my students often depended upon my presentation of the content. I realized that I had to know them in a way that I could address their needs as adolescent students. That meant it was necessary to be meticulous in my planning and consistently reflective in my lessons. If something wasn't working, I started looking at my own teaching strategies instead of immediately blaming the student's poor behavior. That was hard. It wasn't comfortable for me to acknowledge my role in managing my class. However, through this reflective practice, I realized that I needed to learn more about my students' developmental stages and change my approach. I started to understand that extrinsic incentives weren't working because it allowed the students to be passive. I needed to create a classroom environment where students wanted to be engaged.

Classroom management can easily be associated with posters of rules and behavior charts, but it's really about understanding your students so you know what works and what doesn't. Yes, sometimes that might involve a large display of rules or an incentive chart, but those things do not define management. They are simply tools to help your students reach their potential. Classroom management isn't just about fixing unwanted behaviors. A healthy classroom culture can also happen by knowing when to throw your well-planned lesson out the window because it's not working.

KNOW YOUR STUDENTS

It's essential to seek out information about the developmental needs of your students. Whether you teach elementary, middle, or high school students, you can only be responsive to their needs if you know what it is they need in the first place. For example, middle school students experience profound changes during their adolescent years. Because they are growing so fast, they are often uncomfortable in their bodies. This means they might be squirmy in class or wiggle around in their seat. Sometimes they can't even sit for very long at all! Is the difficult student in the back of your class moving around because he is misbehaving, or is he just uncomfortable in his growing body? This is an important distinction because a potentially troublesome student might need to move around a little. Then you can start to reflect on your teaching practice. Is it even realistic to ask them to sit in their chairs for forty minutes? How can you adjust your classroom routine to incorporate movement for this child (and the other adolescent students) in your class? What you might initially think is a bad behavior could in fact just be a symptom of development. How can you use this knowledge for better classroom management? The student's wiggling is no longer an issue because you can be responsive to his need to move and purposefully make movement part of the lesson. The trick is to get curious about the cognitive, physical, and social/emotional development of your students. To be clear, developmental needs are not an excuse for bad behavior, but sometimes we can reframe a bad behavior into a developmental need.

A colleague of mine, Mr. Kay, told me a story about his 5th grade student Jonathan who could not sit still in music class. He would start off wiggling in his seat, until his legs started to move around. Then he couldn't sit anymore and had to stand, and at that point he became a distraction to all of the other students. One day after class, my colleague asked Jonathan why he couldn't sit still. "Music is boring," he said defiantly. So, Mr. Kay asked, "What does being bored feel like in your body?" Jonathan thought for a minute and responded, "Well, my feet feel all stiff and I can't keep them still. And then my knees need to shake and my legs get fuzzy, and I just have to move." And then Mr. Kay had a lightbulb moment: Jonathan was growing! He was having growing pains and couldn't sit still. His behavior "problem" was now a symptom of growing up! Instead of lunch detentions and being sent out of class for distracting the other students, whenever Jonathan's legs felt fuzzy, he was able to take a "hot pass" to go for a short walk and then return to class. Jonathan was no longer a behavior problem, and became an exemplary music student. *That* is classroom management.

Let's take a look at older students. Teenagers in high school are very emotional beings, and although they might look like functioning adults, their brains are *fully* under construction. They have a hard time seeing the long-term value in things they don't understand or that they don't feel are relevant to them (like quadratic equations, or how their choices about social media will affect them in the future). In most situations, they use emotion instead of logic to make decisions. They also crave autonomy because they want to feel as if they have some control in their lives, especially in school where many decisions are made for them.

How can you use this information in the classroom? Give them emotional choices to make! Perhaps they are the ones in charge of adding expressive elements to their songs instead of you. What would happen if you isolated a phrase and took out all of the dynamics and articulation markings so they could put in their own? Music is the perfect avenue for making emotional decisions. In recognizing their need for autonomy, perhaps a teacher standing in front of the ensemble for the whole rehearsal giving directions might not be developmentally responsive. What if a student conducted the ensemble, or led warm-ups? If you think about what the students need cognitively, socially, and emotionally, you can structure your whole class differently.

What are three things you know about the development of the children you are teaching? If you can't answer this right away, do some research about the age level you teach. Consider their cognitive, social, emotional, moral, psychological, and physical growth. This should always inform your teaching practices, particularly regarding classroom management. Use this space for fast facts:

_____

_____

_____

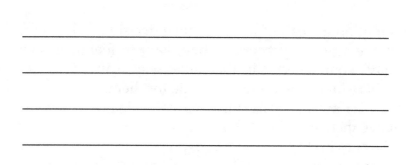

RELATIONSHIPS

Take the time to get to know your students. Really know about them. Building relationships with the kids in your classes will pave the way towards a well-managed classroom. Ask them about their weekend and find out about their hobbies. Sometimes this can be as simple as walking through a rehearsal for a minute or two when they are practicing on their own and asking a student a question about their day, or how they did at their softball game. They will be more connected to you and your class if they feel like you care about them as individuals.

During my guitar unit in 7th grade general music, I start each class with a warm-up song on the board so I can take the time to walk around the room. I pretend that I need to tune all of the guitars at the beginning of class, but it's really just a way to strike up a conversation. They are usually tuned pretty well, but this way I get a chance to connect with each student individually. I ask them about their day, their pets, or if they are ready for the upcoming science test. They share all sorts of things with me in those few moments. I know who just got a baby sister, who went shopping for a new dress for the dance, and who had a tough weekend because their grandma died. While this routine takes a few minutes at the beginning of the period, it can be the most important part of the class for me.

Building these relationships also fosters an atmosphere of belonging. It is so important that the students feel like they belong in your class. This is easy to accomplish in an ensemble with ready-made groups like the horn section, the percussion section, or the soprano section. However, it's very different in a general music class. If students feel as if they belong, they will be more likely to participate, take creative risks, and make positive contributions to the class.

Years ago, my students were getting ready for an upcoming performance as a Ghanaian drumming ensemble. Each year the kids played during halftime at a soccer game at the local community college. It was a big deal. We had two rehearsals left and we needed to clean things up just a little bit. Our bell player, Jarred, was awesome. In a drumming ensemble, the bell is the heartbeat of each song. If the bell isn't right, the whole thing falls apart. Not everyone is able to play the bell for a long period of time, but Jarred never wavered. He was steady and gave us the foundation we needed.

Fourth period started and the kids rushed into class, grabbed their drums and got into place. Everyone except Jarred. He wasn't there. Where was Jarred? We were all worried, and a little nervous about the rehearsal. I knew I would have to play the bell part and speak the master drum part loudly enough so everyone would hear. We had to rehearse, but we felt lost without him there.

About ten minutes into class, Jarred walked through the door. "Jarred!" everyone shouted. "You're here! Get the bell!!" The kids went nuts. They were so excited that he was there. Outside of class, Jarred was quiet. He usually kept to himself and had some trouble navigating through the social warzone of middle school. He was often disengaged and disconnected in school, but in my class, he belonged. On that day, he knew he mattered and we needed him. The joy on his face when he walked in the classroom has stayed with me for years. I strive to provide that same sense of belonging in each of my classes.

ROUTINE AND CONSISTENCY

All students, no matter their age, thrive when they have routine. Let's be honest, we all do better when there is a routine. You can help set students up for success by having a consistent routine with clear expectations. The routine can be as simple as, "Come in to the room, get your instrument, and start warming up," or, "When you enter the room, get your folder and find your seat." It might seem like common sense to you, but the students need to review the expectations once in a while. Depending on your class, you can come up with rules and expectations with your students. This is an exercise many teachers enjoy and have found to be very meaningful. In my experience, it doesn't matter if you make up the rules yourself or if it's a joint effort with the class as long as they are reasonable, clearly understood, and everyone is held accountable, including you.

A seating chart is another helpful way to establish routine. It's much easier when students can just come into your classroom and immediately know where to sit. They don't have to think about it, and they don't have a chance to sit with someone that could cause drama during class. Yes, give them choices every so often as you see fit, but at least for the first few weeks of school, you should decide who sits where. The seating chart is something that will also come in handy at the beginning of the year when you're learning their names. And please...learn their names quickly. They can tell when you don't! When you make this a priority, you begin to develop rapport with the kids right from the start.

Decide beforehand the protocols about coming late to class, disrespectful behavior, and mishandling instruments or equipment. Include rules about leaving the classroom to go to the bathroom, to get a drink, or to go to their locker. Make them short and easy to remember. Keep rules and procedures part of the conversation often as a consistent reminder to everyone. This will help with a potential exodus, where mysteriously every student has to go to the bathroom at the same time.

Here is some space to brainstorm ideas for your classroom expectations:

Bathroom:_____

_____

_____

Locker:_____

_____

_____

Late to class:_____

_____

_____

Disrespectful behavior:_____

_____

_____

Mishandling equipment:_____

_____

_____

LANGUAGE

To help maintain a positive classroom culture, focus on the things the students do well and on the behaviors that exemplify what you want. Praise them for doing the right thing instead of pointing out the unwanted behaviors. "I see 90% of the class doing the right thing," is usually more effective than "I am waiting for you to stop talking, Robyn!" Also, if some students often exhibit challenging behavior, make sure to acknowledge when they are doing the right thing, even if it's small. They need to know that you notice them all of the time, not only when they are doing something they are not supposed to. The negative attention-seeking behavior might diminish once they realize they can get attention for following the rules.

Be sure to hold the students to the same expectation of positive, encouraging language. Every so often, a class gets a little chatty and one well-meaning student yells, "Shut up!" to everyone. Because I find those words cringe-worthy, I use it as a teachable moment. Although the intentions might have been good, I shine a light on the importance of being kind to each other.

Classroom culture isn't just about how you speak to the students and manage behavior. It's also about how they interact with each other.

Once I had a new student come into class when we were in the middle of our Ghanaian drumming unit. During this lesson, the students were split up into smaller groups working on the rhythms they had learned. The new student looked a little shy and sat down with a group of boys who were practicing. He clearly felt intimidated and looked as if he didn't want to hit the drum the wrong way, so he didn't touch it at all. One of the boys was very encouraging and kind and said to him "We'll teach you. Just play something. We won't judge you if you make a mistake." My heart was full. Our language really makes a difference and can set a good example for your students.

READING THE ROOM

Classroom management is also about reading the room. Sometimes the lesson that took so much time to plan just won't work. Let it go and change gears. You need to have a keen sense of how your lesson is being received. After my experience in college and student teaching, I expected all of my future students to be compliant to my every academic challenge and grateful for the lessons I spent hours creating. This is not reality. They don't care how long you worked on a lesson for them.

If you are feeling stuck with a particular class, movement can help. A change in physical state can have a huge effect on focus and attention. Figure out a way to turn your activity into something where they can move. When the students begin to move around, the whole energy of the room can change. These kids sit in class most of the day so it is important to get them up and moving. (Even in a high school band rehearsal.)

Every spring, my 7th and 8th grade students take standardized tests. They sit for these exams for two hours and then continue on with the rest of their day. One year I had my junior high chorus (of sixty kids) right after the testing. I knew that my lesson was not going to work, and if I stayed with my original plan, it would have been a disaster. So instead, I started class with a call-and-response exercise using body percussion. They were so focused on my combinations of snaps, claps, stomps, and vocalizing that it became a game. I made it more difficult as it went along. I completely had their attention. It was really helpful to get them using their pent up energy in a positive and productive way.

Most days my kids are focused and ready to work. However, once in a while their energy is either extremely hyper or very lethargic. On these days, if I were to stick to my regular routine the students would not be very successful. While I usually use lots of movement throughout rehearsal anyway, these special days call for me to incorporate even more. If I notice it's a particularly high-energy day, I will start class with slow stretches and mindful breathing to help regain focus. On seemingly sleepy days, I use lots of body percussion during warm-ups. I also use a warm-up that includes a full body shake. The students shake each hand one at a time and then each foot for ten, nine, eight, seven, six, five, four, three, two, one; then nine, eight, seven, six, five, four, three, two, one; eight, seven, six, five, four, three, two, one, etc. This small exercise is equivalent to hitting the reset button on their brains for better focus!

It's so important to ask yourself, "What do they need today?" and lean into that need. Sometimes these classes end up being the most successful and a lot of fun. Build a toolbox of lessons and activities for when you're in a pinch. If something isn't working, stop and think. Consider if the circumstance or lack of focus calls for a consequence, or if they just need a brain break instead. This can be as easy as a quick stretch in the middle of rehearsal.

WHEN THEY DON'T MAKE GOOD CHOICES

When a student makes a bad decision, it's important to ask him, "Why do you think you made that choice?" Sometimes the answer will be, "I don't know." If we are continuing to reframe behavior as developmental symptoms, it's necessary to remember that their brains have not fully developed yet. The prefrontal cortex (PFT) is the part of the brain that is responsible for many functions including decision-making, prioritizing, organization, and anticipating consequences. It does not fully develop until we're in our early to mid-twenties. That's right...in our twenties! As a result, it is not always possible for our students to articulate the reason they made a poor choice.

Keep the conversation going so they can think about what's going on. Is the student hungry? Tired? Stressed? Did something happen at lunch with a friend? Is a parent or loved one sick? Is he experiencing sensory overload? Was he just being impulsive? Literally anything can provoke a student to make a poor choice, but it's up to you to take a moment to find out what's really going on.

You must practice responding to what is happening instead of reacting to it. If a student is causing you to feel frustrated or angry, take a breath and pause. In order to prevent escalating a situation, you need to have a keen sense of self-awareness. Notice how you are feeling, breathe, and then continue the conversation. This small moment of pause will allow you the space to decide how to handle something rationally. You will not be able to do this well if your emotions are getting the better of you in the moment.

Sometimes, they still won't do the right thing. You want the students to make good choices all of the time, so you give them a chance. Then another one. And then one more. You know they know how to do the right thing, so again...one more chance. Before you know it, that one student has held the class hostage with his or her bad behavior. This scenario is all too common, especially among newer teachers. Dignify your rules and classroom expectations with following through. If your behavior policies still aren't working, set up a meeting with the student, guidance counselor, principal and/or parent.

You must always mean what you say and say what you mean. If you tell a student that you will contact their parent, make sure you do. If you want them to stay with you during lunch and they don't show, request the help of a guidance counselor or other teacher to hold him or her accountable for the earned consequence. If you don't follow through, you will lose your credibility and the kids will be on to you!

In the end, don't take their bad behavior personally (even though I know this is incredibly easy for me to say to you and I, myself, have taken lots of things personally over the years). So okay, yes, you will probably take some of these poor choices and bad behavior personally, but keep reminding yourself not to. Bad behavior most often has nothing to do with you. If you dig a little deeper, you might find a heartbreaking reason that's causing their poor choices. When students are at their worst, there is usually something else happening underneath the angry facade. When they act out, get curious. Ask them what's going on. It can be as simple as, "I can see you're not yourself today. Are you okay?" Or, "Tell me what's going on with you today. I can see that you're feeling frustrated." Sometimes they just need someone to talk to.

Other times they will try to get you to engage in a power struggle. This is when a student becomes defiant or insubordinate and wants to gain control over a situation. For example, after numerous warnings, you ask the student to take a break in the back of the room. He then says, "No." Don't ever get into a power struggle. Just don't. You won't win. In those situations, it's important to keep your cool and maintain a great deal of self-regulation. You have to stay calm in order to deal with a difficult student effectively. In this scenario, it is helpful to engage the rest class in an activity so you can speak with him privately. When you are baited with a power struggle, take a deep breath, assess the situation, and get curious.

I once had a student first period that would constantly give me a hard time. First thing in the morning Marc was defiant and grumpy. I finally asked him what was going on. "Are you okay? Every morning you seem angry. Are mornings tough for you?" He told me that many days he comes a little bit late to school and he misses the free breakfast. He was hungry! His behavior wasn't about me or my music class. When I got curious about the choices he was making, I discovered how I could help. From then on, I kept some granola bars and other small breakfast foods in my office for him. If he was late to school and missed breakfast, he knew he could have something to eat before he joined my class. After I figured it out on that day, I saw a complete turnaround in his behavior.

When you've asked all the questions and still

can't seem to find the reason behind the behavior, you may need a different approach. You have to understand that you can't actually make the students do anything. When there is a conflict and the student is feeling stubborn, give them choices. Sometimes this surprises them. They are so used to adults telling them what to do that when you give them a choice, they are usually caught off guard. Here's how this can work:

Student 1

Kim keeps talking to her neighbors, making it difficult for anyone to concentrate. Instead of demanding that she move her seat, say, "I can see that you are distracted today. Are you doing okay?" (Her answer might surprise you). "You can either move your seat so you can focus, or take some time in the back of the classroom to reset and come back when you're ready. What would you like to do?"

Student 2

Jamie has taken his phone out again after his first warning to put it away. Calmly say, "Jamie I can see you are on your phone again. You can either give me your phone until the end of the day and pick it up before you leave, or you can keep it and I will contact your parents to tell them you were using your phone during my class. Which would you prefer?"

In these scenarios, there are consequences either way but the student gets to choose. Giving them choices lets them have some sense of control and autonomy. (Be sure these are choices where you can follow through!) Of course, it's possible that a situation might arise that does not warrant a choice and a student's behavior earns them a trip to the office. Make sure you are familiar with your school's behavior policies so you can be consistent with everyone else. Hopefully, this will be rare. If they are able to choose their consequence and their behavior is still a problem, then it is in your hands to make a decision. They should understand that choice too. Help them recognize that it was their choice that brought on this consequence. When your expectations are clear, there isn't a lot of room for interpretation. Even asking throughout class, "Does everyone understand the expectation?" is helpful.

Kids can feel embarrassed very easily, so when you address the behavior of an individual student, try to be discreet. Whenever possible, talk to the student causing the disruption while the other students are busy doing another task. Sometimes you don't even have to say anything to address a behavior problem. Move around the classroom. Even your proximity to a student can change an unwanted behavior.

At the end of the day, it's important to remember that if they are making bad choices, you aren't failing them. Instead, they are failing to meet your expectations. This is sometimes the hardest thing to accept as a new teacher. You are told throughout your pre-service training in college that every student should be able to find success in your class. Yes, you should absolutely provide an opportunity for every student to succeed. Every student certainly has the potential to do well. However, if a student is sabotaging your class and the other students are unable to learn, then you need to address that student's behavior. If he is dealing with issues at home or on the school yard, he might not be ready to learn in class. Maybe that day the lesson you teach that student is about self-regulation or self-control. For a student with frequent behavior challenges, talk with the guidance counselors and reach out to his other teachers. Have a conversation with the student's parents or guardians sooner rather than later. More likely than not, if a student is a challenge in your class, he is having difficulties in his other classes as well.

When it comes to discipline, I always think back to Mary Poppins' description of herself as "kind, but extremely firm." I love that and try to live this philosophy as best as I can. I have heard my students say, "Mrs. Rafferty doesn't yell; she sternly says." Some days it might feel tempting to raise your voice, but most often, this is not an effective way to get your students to do what you ask. Yelling fosters feelings of anger, guilt, and shame. These emotions are not fitting for a classroom that should be inspiring. When you yell, the students generally just hear your voice, not your words. Use the volume and delivery of your words wisely so you can appropriately respond to their actions.

EMPOWERING THEM TO MAKE GOOD CHOICES

Remember that discipline is not about the student's character, but about his or her choices. There is a large difference between, "You are foolish," and, "What you did was foolish." The second statement leaves room for change and does not define students by the choices they made.

An important key to classroom management is empowering students to understand that they can change their choices. If they believe that they are bad, it is a lot easier for them to perpetuate that story by being a "bad kid" who is defined by their bad choices. On the other hand, when you emphasize the choice, as in, "You made a poor choice when you were disrespectful to the instruments," this gives them space to make a different choice. As teachers we help mold the stories that the students tell themselves about who they are. Music teachers in particular need to be mindful of our language. The same idea also goes for positive reinforcement. Praise the deed instead of the doer. This will encourage more good-deed-doing because good choices are concrete and attainable.

IF YOU STILL FEEL STUCK

Classroom management is something new teachers can easily get stuck on. We put so much stock into our students' success that when they misbehave, don't participate, and say things that are hurtful, it can be like a punch to the gut. It's hard not to take it personally. When you have a rough day at school, go home, recharge, and try again the next day. You can't give something you don't have, so if you are not feeling inspired, the students probably aren't feeling it either! Start with a clean slate each morning for both you and your students.

5.
THE "A" WORD
(ASSESSMENT)

"Children must be taught how to think,
not what to think." ~ Margaret Mead

The word "assessment" usually evokes some feelings. Music teachers at many different stages in their careers have told me that the word "assessment" often brings up cringe-worthy feelings of nausea, stress, and anxiety. Others, however, have described assessments as making them feel empowered, accomplished, and even excited. This stark difference was fascinating to me. I started to dig a little deeper as to why people had such opposing responses to this word. It seemed that the reason for these two emotional camps had to do with a fundamental understanding (or misunderstanding) of what assessments are and what they can be.

To be honest, I used to feel anxiety and stress about that word. When I first started teaching, I had trouble wrapping my head around it. Why do we have to assess students at all in music? I was a music teacher, not a math teacher! I knew they were learning because I heard them and witnessed their growth. What kind of assessment would enhance my class instead of take away from our valuable rehearsal time? And besides, music is subjective, right? I can't just give an A to the best performing students!

Part of our job as their teacher is to determine whether or not the students are indeed understanding the information we are teaching. Music class should be a place for fun and creative expression, but we also need to make sure they learn something. Since our discipline is a performance-based subject, pencil-and-paper assessments usually aren't the most authentic way to assess, although they can be useful at times. In the music classroom we can tell if they are learning because we can see and hear them, but often this information needs to be communicated in a way that makes sense to the students, parents, and administrators (which sometimes means a number or letter grade). Before we dig into how to do this, let's first unpack the question, "What are assessments?"

Generally, there are two types of assessments: formative and summative. Formative assessments monitor the progress of the students as a lesson or lessons unfold. Summative assessments happen at the end of a unit of learning, are evaluative, and usually attached to a grade

In a music class, formative assessments are used all the time. Because we listen to our students minute to minute, we are constantly assessing during rehearsal. For example, we notice if the students are playing a scale accurately, singing a melody with the right rhythms, or if they are able to recognize fast versus slow. This kind of assessment throughout the rehearsal should not be graded, as it will only be used to inform your teaching practices. Then you will be able to adjust the lesson according to what you hear. You might need to review the sharps of the A scale, go over the rhythms again, or use a different exercise with the kindergartners so they can hear fast and slow. Formative assessments are already built into what we do as music educators because we are always listening. This is good news! Throughout class, you should have a consistent understanding of how your students are doing.

Summative assessments evaluate the student's knowledge at the end of a unit. In an ensemble there aren't really units in the same way we might recognize a science unit or even a unit in general music. However, there should be places throughout the year where you can use summative assessments based on a standard. These can be district or department standards and should also align with the state or national standards.

WHAT CAN ASSESSMENT LOOK LIKE?

Here are some examples that you can use as either formative or summative assessments for a music classroom. This is not by any means an exhaustive list but will hopefully give you some other ideas about how to assess students in a way that aligns with your school grading policies and your teaching philosophy:

Rubrics: When I first started teaching, I underestimated the value of a rubric. It took a while for me to see how important this tool can be, particularly how it can hold students accountable for their own learning. The rubric should be given at the same time you tell your students about the assignment or an upcoming graded performance so they can understand the expectations. Refer to it often, and check in with their progress for each item throughout the process. If your class is large, a one-on-one conversation isn't always necessary or practical. Sometimes a "thumbs-up, thumbs-down" check-in is all that needs to happen for you to get a general handle on their understanding.

For the rubric, choose just a few essential standards that are the core of what they should master by the time they have completed the task.

Here is an example of a rubric on the following page that can be used for a graded performance in a general music class. The task was to create a composition in groups using ABA form and perform for the class.

As the students get more familiar with using rubrics, have them choose their own learning objectives. Whenever students are able to have a voice and a choice in their experiences at school, the more relevant the learning becomes. Give them a chance to make their own rubric.

This is also a great opportunity to reach out to other teachers. It might be a good idea to use a rubric format similar to those used in other classes because consistency is important for the students.

Learning Objective/ Standard	4	3	2	1
Demonstrates understanding of ADA form	Very clear A section and contrasting B section.	Somewhat clear A section and/or B section not as contrasting.	A and B section did not have much contrast at all.	No clear A or B section, or did not create an ABA pattern.
Performing	Performed with confidence and accuracy.	Performed with moderate confidence. Could have used a little more practice.	Did not know the part very well. Much more practice needed.	Inaccurate performance.
Tempo	Steady beat was consistent throughout.	Beat was somewhat steady. Some places were not together with the rest of the group.	The beat was not together but did not distract from the overall performance.	The beat was inconsistent and took away from the performance.
Work with others	Worked very well with the other members of the group. No redirection needed.	Worked moderately well with the group. Some redirection was necessary to remain on task.	Had difficulty working in the group without consistent help from the teacher.	Did not work well with the group.

Self-Assessment: This allows the students a chance to actively think about their learning. How do they think they are doing? What have they learned? What is easy for them? What is challenging? What is their next step for further understanding? When you involve students in this reflection, you empower them to realize their role in their learning. They should be seeking and discovering knowledge for their own understanding.

Self-assessments can come in many forms and should be age appropriate. Listed below are three different examples of self-assessments I have used over the years for elementary, junior and senior high. Use these in your class, or adapt them to meet the needs of your teaching situation.

Self-Assessment Rubric: I often have my rubric double-sided so the students can do a self-assessment using the same rubric. This gives them a chance to reflect on their learning process as it aligns with my grading expectations.

Traffic Light: This is a great informal way to use a formative assessment. With a simple chart of "Got it!" "Almost," and "Not Yet," a student can clip on a clothespin with her name on it. This is an easy visual for you to get an idea of how the class is doing with any concept. The students can then use it for motivation to set goals to improve and move their clothespin after the next class. Since this is not a private type of assessment, do not use this as a tool for teacher feedback. This should just be used as a self-assessment by the students about their own learning.

Number Scale: This self-assessment allows the students to rate themselves on a continuum. Sometimes I ask them to respond about their content knowledge. Other times, I have them assess themselves on basic class routines. This can easily be adapted for younger students with emojis for them to circle. Here are a few ideas:

Circle one (1- never 5- always)

1. I come to class on time, prepared and ready to learn.
   1 2 3 4 5

2. I can sight-read a rhythmic pattern with quarter notes and eighth notes.
   1 2 3 4 5

3. I am a leader in my section by listening to directions during rehearsal.
   1 2 3 4 5

4. I ask questions when I am unsure of something.
   1 2 3 4 5

Technology: If technology is available to you, use it. We live in a world where students are constantly plugged in and online. Use their desire to get on a device and incorporate it in their assessments. There are many ways to create assessments using technology. Student recordings are a great way to listen at a later time and assess performances. You can even listen (or watch) with the student and explain your feedback. This can be an extremely valuable way for students to hear their own performance because they often hear themselves differently in the moment.

There are also many programs available for all sorts of assessments. To keep your class relevant, it's essential that you incorporate technology whenever possible. The following resources have been helpful for me over the years and there are many more out there. Use them as tools to make assessments more authentic and engaging for students. As I am writing this, I realize that some of these programs will probably be outdated eventually. Although, I will wager that the internet will be around for a while, so they are worth mentioning now:

SmartMusic: This is a great program for student performance assessments. It is perfect for guided practice and gives immediate feedback on their performance.

GarageBand/Soundtrap: GarageBand is an Apple app that provides the opportunity to create, record, mix, and arrange all sorts of music. Soundtrap is similar, but it is internet-based and can be accessed through any device.

Noteflight/Finale/Sibelius: These are all composition programs for students to write their own music.

Google Classroom: Stay connected with your students through this platform. Lessons, articles, discussion boards, and many different kinds of assessments can all be put into your virtual classroom so students can access them through any device. Many of the other programs mentioned above can also be linked into an assignment on Google Classroom. No more loose papers!

Large Class Assessments: In an ensemble setting, it can be challenging to figure out an appropriate assessment because there are so many students in your class at the same time. For some types of assessments it can be helpful to have a large seating chart with checkboxes (Yes, Almost, Not Yet) so you can walk around the room as they play, sing or demonstrate whatever the assignment was. You can then check off the appropriate box so you can have data of who is mastering the standard, who is almost meeting the standard, and those who are not quite there yet. We usually have this information in our heads as we listen throughout a rehearsal, but documentation is very helpful. This data can also be used to look at your students' achievements in a way that is more concrete. To take it a step further, the students can fill out the same checkboxes each day so they can monitor their own progress. This should also inform instruction for the next lesson. Can you teach something differently? Is there an opportunity to have students learn from each other in pairs or in small groups? What if the students who are mastering a standard had some leadership roles in class as they helped other students?

Here are two examples of what this could look like. The first is for an early elementary general music classroom followed by one that could be used in a high school ensemble setting. You can use the second chart by cutting out the squares to make individual papers for students to assess themselves on how they did on a particular day. This could also work as an exit ticket as they leave the classroom.

Standard: Differentiate between high and low tones
Date:

Sam ❏ Yes ❏ Almost ❏ Not Yet	Mike ❏ Yes ❏ Almost ❏ Not Yet	Molly ❏ Yes ❏ Almost ❏ Not Yet	Ted ❏ Yes ❏ Almost ❏ Not Yet
Chris ❏ Yes ❏ Almost ❏ Not Yet	Jake ❏ Yes ❏ Almost ❏ Not Yet	Sandra ❏ Yes ❏ Almost ❏ Not Yet	Rebecca ❏ Yes ❏ Almost ❏ Not Yet
Kim ❏ Yes ❏ Almost ❏ Not Yet	Aurora ❏ Yes ❏ Almost ❏ Not Yet	Rachel ❏ Yes ❏ Almost ❏ Not Yet	Kevin ❏ Yes ❏ Almost ❏ Not Yet
Janice ❏ Yes ❏ Almost ❏ Not Yet	Philip ❏ Yes ❏ Almost ❏ Not Yet	Kelsey ❏ Yes ❏ Almost ❏ Not Yet	Ethan ❏ Yes ❏ Almost ❏ Not Yet

Sam
I can play my part with accurate articulations and phrasing.
❏ Yes
❏ Almost
❏ Not Yet

Mike
I can play my part with accurate articulations and phrasing.
❏ Yes
❏ Almost
❏ Not Yet

Molly
I can play my part with accurate articulations and phrasing.
❏ Yes
❏ Almost
❏ Not Yet

Ted
I can play my part with accurate articulations and phrasing.
❏ Yes
❏ Almost
❏ Not Yet

Chris
I can play my part with accurate articulations and phrasing.
❏ Yes
❏ Almost
❏ Not Yet

Jake
I can play my part with accurate articulations and phrasing.
❏ Yes
❏ Almost
❏ Not Yet

Sandra
I can play my part with accurate articulations and phrasing.
❏ Yes
❏ Almost
❏ Not Yet

Rebecca
I can play my part with accurate articulations and phrasing.
❏ Yes
❏ Almost
❏ Not Yet

Kim
I can play my part with accurate articulations and phrasing.
❏ Yes
❏ Almost
❏ Not Yet

Aurora
I can play my part with accurate articulations and phrasing.
❏ Yes
❏ Almost
❏ Not Yet

Rachel
I can play my part with accurate articulations and phrasing.
❏ Yes
❏ Almost
❏ Not Yet

Kevin
I can play my part with accurate articulations and phrasing.
❏ Yes
❏ Almost
❏ Not Yet

Janice
I can play my part with accurate articulations and phrasing.
❏ Yes
❏ Almost
❏ Not Yet

Philip
I can play my part with accurate articulations and phrasing.
❏ Yes
❏ Almost
❏ Not Yet

Kelsey
I can play my part with accurate articulations and phrasing.
❏ Yes
❏ Almost
❏ Not Yet

Ethan
I can play my part with accurate articulations and phrasing.
❏ Yes
❏ Almost
❏ Not Yet

Stations: When my son was in preschool, his classroom was set up with lots of stations. He had a block station, imaginative play station, coloring station, and a sensory station. It occurred to me that this might be an interesting way to approach my general music class. I started to use stations to have the students rotate through instruments so I could hear them in small groups. Once the students were proficient enough, I had them move around the room in their groups. I set up a bass station, guitar chord station, TAB station, piano station, and two pen-and-paper stations for completing a self-assessment and to write out guitar chords. The students loved the change of pace and new structure of the class. It also gave them the opportunity to get up and move around as they went from place to place.

Portfolios: This is a good way to see a student's work over time. Create checkpoints frequently so you can monitor student understanding. Portfolios provide students a chance to take on a large part of the responsibility for their own learning because they need to have a completed, cumulative project at the end of the year or semester. This allows you the flexibility to give assignments over a period of time (critiques, self-assessments, reflections, rhythm and note reading, repertoire, etc.). At the end of the year the students will have something meaningful to take home with them.

Use the space below to start brainstorming ways that you can incorporate these assessments in your classes. Be specific. What will they look like? What is the standard that you want to assess? Determine if this will be a formative or summative assessment.

Assessment 1
Formative or Summative?

_____

What standard/skill are you assessing?

_____

_____

_____

What are the student's expectations?
(What will she have to do?)

_____

_____

_____

How will the students know if they have mastered the standard/skill?

_____

_____

_____

Assessment 2
Formative or Summative?

_____

What standard/skill are you assessing?

_____

_____

_____

What are the student's expectations?
(What will she have to do?)

_____

_____

_____

How will the students know if they have mastered the standard/skill?

_____

_____

_____

Assessment 3
Formative or Summative?

_____

What standard/skill are you assessing?

_____

_____

_____

What are the student's expectations?
(What will she have to do?)

_____

_____

_____

How will the students know if they have mastered the standard/skill?

_____

_____

_____

FEEDBACK

Whichever way you decide to assess your class, remember that your feedback is the most important part. This is your opportunity to communicate to your students what went well, what didn't, and how they can improve. Feedback should be kind, specific, and helpful. Before the assessment, be clear as to what their feedback will be about. Will the feedback simply be evaluative (a grade), acknowledgement and appreciation of completing the task, or will you provide some coaching? Most of the time, it will be a combination of these three things.

Keep in mind, you don't have to be the only person delivering feedback. Consider incorporating assessments where students can give feedback to each other. This is a great way for them to practice the language of constructive feedback. I am sure you can remember a time when a student commented about another student's performance with something along the lines of, "You played okay, but you messed up a lot." This is not kind, specific, or helpful, and probably had a negative impact on the student who was performing. Giving some attention and practice to the language of feedback provides an opportunity to learn this very important skill. Students at every age are capable of giving great feedback which will in turn make them better at receiving it.

It's easy to use phrases such as "I liked it!" or, "It was great!" While their intentions might be positive and encouraging, these are very subjective and basic comments. In my classes, instead of giving feedback that begins with "I liked," or "I didn't like," I encourage them to say "I noticed," "I wonder," and "I wish." This idea has come from many different sources, but it is very clear in Amy Burvall and Dan Ryder's book *Intention: Critical Creativity in the Classroom.*

"I noticed" is for something they thought went really well. For example, "I noticed your crescendo was very smooth," or "I noticed that you enjoyed performing because your face showed a lot of excitement when you were singing." Using feedback in this way removes the subjective nature of the responses and allows the student to be very specific with their communication. To be clear, it is also important for the students to acknowledge something they really liked; however, the feedback has to go deeper than that.

"I wonder" is for a suggestion to improve something that is almost working well. If their phrasing was a little awkward, appropriate feedback could be "I wonder what would happen if you found places to take breaths that allowed the phrases to be more fluid." The "I wonder" phrase is a great way to get the students to give their creative input without necessarily telling someone what to do.

"I wish" is used for something that didn't go very well. For example, "I wish those tricky measures were more accurate. Perhaps you could spend a few minutes isolating that section and practice it more slowly." In this example, the feedback meets the kind, specific and helpful requirements without saying, "Wow, those six measures were a mess!" Using "I wish" creates a safe, non-judgmental space to give and receive constructive feedback.

This language does not come naturally. I have to constantly be mindful of the words I use for feedback, and now my students remind me when I forget! Especially at the beginning, it is important to give frequent reminders to everyone in the room about the feedback expectations. However, once the kids (and you) get the hang of it, they will have a tremendous advantage in other areas of their lives in both giving and receiving feedback.

6.
MUSIC FOR EVERY STUDENT

*"Educating the mind without educating the heart is
no education at all." ~ Aristotle*

As a music teacher, you should always be prepared
for advocacy. When the school's financial waistband
is getting too tight or scheduling becomes difficult to
figure out, music is too often considered something
extra or expendable. Coming out of college, I was
armed with the knowledge that a music education is
an essential part of every student's school experience.
Participation in music fosters lifelong skills that reach
far beyond the music classroom. It wasn't until I started
teaching that I came to realize that many people did
not share my perspective.

When you think of advocacy, you might imagine
a call to action at a school board meeting packed with
parents and community members. Pictures may come
to mind of students pleading with administrators to
save their music program, sharing stories about how
music has taught them so much about themselves and

they couldn't imagine life without it. In this scene, angry and assertive parents speak on behalf of the music department trying to convince the decision makers that music is a necessary part of their child's education, and should be highly regarded in every school district.

While this type of dramatic advocacy happens, it is sometimes too little, too late. Meaningful advocacy occurs every day, and as a music teacher, you have a lot of power in advocating for your program. Advocacy does not happen only at a meeting in the eleventh hour before the school board makes an important financial decision. Advocacy is about educating your students, fellow teachers, administrators, and community members about the importance of music education all of the time. This is something that music teachers take for granted because we know this already! Of course music is important! It's common sense to us! Unfortunately, that knowledge can be to our detriment because it results in an inaccurate assumption that everyone knows these things. They don't.

The language of advocacy takes practice and will take time for fluency. It is especially challenging because when you have conversations advocating for your program, you are generally talking with someone who does not have a background in music, someone who has an agenda that may not be in your best interest, or someone who does not have an understanding about what we do as music teachers. It's possible that they fall into all three of these categories. It is so important to remember that you need to educate while you advocate.

Sometimes you might find yourself in a situation that requires immediate explanations about why music should be in school, reasons for pull-out lessons, or reasons why ensembles shouldn't be scheduled during recess. Your words can easily escape you during these unexpected or high-pressure interactions. I was one time stopped on the way to the bathroom by a principal telling me about a potential change in the schedule that would affect my program. Talk about thinking on my toes! While I didn't go into great detail about the monumental importance of maintaining our program the way it was, I requested that we set up a meeting to talk about it later instead of standing in the hallway in front of the bathroom!

Many music teachers find themselves asking why music education needs defending and explaining. Nobody questions the math teacher as to why schools should teach math during the school day! While these questions are valid, they aren't helpful. Circling around those thoughts is counterproductive, and causes more stress and aggravation. You must remember that you cannot control what other people think or say. What you do have control over is how you respond, how you educate, and how you consistently demonstrate how music is essential for your students.

Advocacy is a tall order, and believe me, it can feel stressful and sometimes deflating. Even as I write these paragraphs, I am noticing a change in my blood pressure. This is something music teachers just have to deal with as a part of our discipline. If you're lucky, you are in a school that honors and celebrates music, trusts that their teachers know what they are doing, and allows the program to grow based on the needs of their students. But, every music teacher in every district will eventually need to advocate for some aspect of the program.

REACTIVE ADVOCACY

Once in a district where I was working, there was a possibility that the band and orchestra were going to be scheduled in the same room at the same time. When I brought it to the attention of my administrators and guidance counselors, they simply suggested that either the band or the orchestra could rehearse in the auditorium. I calmly explained that our auditorium was not a great space for class, especially because we just had a capital project completed and we had a brand new large ensemble room to use. There were also frequent meetings and assemblies that took place in the auditorium throughout the year that would disrupt rehearsals. I needed to take a step back and realize that while this seemed like common sense to me, it was not clear to the administrators. I had many meetings explaining the importance of using the large ensemble space in a way my administrators eventually understood. After another few looks at the master schedule, they were finally able to make a couple of adjustments which would allow for both ensembles to use the large ensemble room at different times.

This type of on-the-spot advocacy is what I refer to as *reactive advocacy*. Reactive advocacy is not fun. It happens when there is a situation that requires some type of triage from you and the rest of your department. For example, a position is potentially being cut; there is a threat to pull-out lessons; or someone decided that you do not need planning time. Whatever the situation, it is extremely helpful to have some ideas ready to go when and if you need to explain the importance of your program and justify what you do.

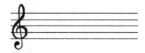

Here is an example:

Problem - Potential elimination of pull-out lessons

Justification - Lessons are necessary for students to learn how to play their instrument. There is a large number of students in band and in order for them to play and read at a level that would make them successful in the ensemble, they need small group lessons.

Solutions - We will provide short, twenty minute lessons. There will also be a rotating schedule so students won't be pulled-out of the same class more than once every six to seven weeks. The music teachers will always communicate with the classroom teachers so everyone knows the schedule. If there is a problem with a specific class or time, we can address it with that individual student.

Use this space for other issues or questions that are specific to your program. Brainstorm your thoughts:

Problem:

_____

_____

_____

Justification:

_____

_____

_____

Solutions:

_____

_____

_____

Get familiar with the words you wrote for the justification and actually practice saying them out loud to a friend or colleague. This might sound silly, but when your principal or other administrator asks you a high-stakes question, I promise that you will be better prepared with the words already there. We are musicians; we understand practice. Don't underestimate the power of being calm, cool, and collected during a high-pressure situation, especially as a newer teacher. Be articulate and informative and remember that facts and numbers are helpful for administrators. Here is a chart to get you started. This is very general, but work with the numbers that best fit your situation. If it's applicable to your program, do this by grade level as well. Fill in your own data from your department:

Total Students in School			
Students in Music		Percentage of Students in Music	
Students in Band		Percentage of Students in Band	
Students in Orchestra		Percentage of Students in Orchestra	
Students in Chorus		Percentage of Students in Chorus	
Students in Band/Chorus		Percentage of Students in Band/Chorus	
Students in Orchestra/Chorus		Percentage of Students in Orchestra/Chorus	
Students in Music Theory		Percentage of Students in Music Theory	

SITUATIONAL ADVOCACY

I define *situational advocacy* as a need to ask for something that would benefit your program and your students. For example, you might need to advocate for smaller general music class size, to make chorus part of the school day instead of during recess, or to improve scheduling to make music courses accessible for more students. This type of advocacy is for situations that are exceedingly inconvenient or not conducive to your circumstances but are not necessarily an emergency.

When you need to ask for something, it is extremely important that you are kind and patient. Remember, the person with whom you are speaking probably does not understand your needs and will not even know what questions to ask for a better understanding. You might have to break things down into small steps, but definitely be mindful of your tone. You do not want to seem pretentious or condescending.

It's helpful to write a proposal. Go through the reasons why the change needs to happen, along with potential obstacles and solutions. Going to an administrator without a few solutions is a sure way to not get what you want. Use the chart you created from the section above and be prepared with answers to potential follow-up questions. When you speak, advocate for your students and not for you. It is a small difference, but it is more meaningful (and hopefully more accurate) when you explain that your students will benefit from this change. After all, advocacy should always be about the students.

PROACTIVE ADVOCACY

The third type of advocacy is *proactive advocacy*. This is the long-range advocacy that takes commitment and time. Proactive advocacy can be extremely powerful. It is about communicating a consistent message to your school and greater community through your words and your actions. You are in charge of the story that is told about your program. You get to write the narrative about how your students and community benefit from music education.

At the same time as we teach our content, we must teach our students about the value of their music education. What does music do for them and for their future selves? As their teachers, we take this knowledge for granted, but it needs to be explicitly explained. How does the community currently value music education? How can you elevate their understanding and give them the language they need to become music advocates themselves? Sometimes it's just about a short, consistent, and repeated message, reminding people that what we do is extremely important. Use your *why* for inspiration.

This type of advocacy can be done in many ways. Here are just a few ideas:

• Personally invite administrators and other VIPs to concerts. The concert dates are probably on the district calendar, but receiving a personal invitation is very special. Sending an invitation also gives the message that you specifically want them to be there. Invite school board members, retired music teachers, or other music patrons in the community. These people are sometimes the ones with the loudest voices regarding policies within the school. Ask them to come and see the results of their investment in your music program.

• Infographics (graphics with information on them) can easily go in programs or in the local newspaper for parents or community members to read. There are free online resources that take you through the steps to create one. Emphasize the importance of a music education and make a call to action to participate in the school program.

• Use the district social media platform, newsletters, and other school communications to share the exciting things happening in your class and the music department. Have a clear understanding about the district's privacy policies regarding student pictures. Use the school websites and social media accounts instead of your own to keep a safe space between your personal and professional social media activity. Share upcoming events, and highlight the things you are doing in your classroom.

• Enlist the help of the tech department or audio-visual staff to help create a video about what your students do in music classes. If your school has an A-V program, this is a great opportunity for a cross-curricular experience for your students. Show the video to everyone at an assembly, a concert, or during homeroom. Give your students a chance to show off their talents and shine a light on the process behind the concerts. Often the only thing that the community sees is the final concert, but we know that the performance is just the tip of the iceberg. The amount of preparation is enormous, so find ways to showcase that process.

• Reach out to a reporter from the local newspaper to cover stories about the music department. Ask them to write a story about an upcoming performance, special event, or to highlight something in your classroom.

• Get in touch with a radio host from a local radio station. Have your kids perform or go in for an interview about an upcoming event. They are always looking for positive news stories. This is a great way for the community to know about your music class. (And it's super cool to be on the radio!)

• Look for opportunities to invite community members into class during the day. For example, host a "Bring Your Parent to Rehearsal Day." Students are responsible to teach a song (singing or playing) to their parent, relative, or another special person in their life. Invite these special guests into your classroom to participate in making music together. If possible, have them perform at a concert.

• Set up student performances in the community. For instance, senior citizen facilities are always looking for activities for their residents and love when young people come in to perform. Find out what's happening in the community and ask if your students can perform in tandem with those events. This can be very powerful and establish the music program as an integral part of the community. Avoid situations where performances will be background music, as it can send the wrong message. If people are chatting and mingling instead of listening to the music, it can actually devalue the importance of the performance and have an opposite effect.

• Give a presentation at a board meeting about what is going well. Have students perform to show off the amazing work that they are doing in class and speak about their experiences in the music program. The music is usually a nice reprieve in the middle of a board meeting.

This list is far from complete. Use this space to brainstorm ideas on how to share the message about the importance of music education. What are some community events or venues that would be appropriate partnerships in this advocacy endeavor?

_____

_____

_____

_____

_____

_____

Also consider that music teachers have a meaningful platform for advocacy every time there is a concert. Use it to educate your parents and greater community about the benefits of music education. Talk to your audience before, during, or after the concerts. You can help reframe how the community views your music program. As a result, when it comes time for the district to make cuts to the budget, no one would even consider reducing funding for the music department.

7.
EQUIP YOUR ROOM FOR SUCCESS

"An investment in knowledge pays the best interest."
~ Benjamin Franklin

When I first started teaching, I soon realized that I had a lot of ideas but not enough equipment (or budget) to do what I wanted. In addition to my choirs, I was teaching general music, and the previous teacher left me with only ten tubano drums, eight guitars, and just a few other auxiliary percussion instruments. I had a great West African drumming unit that I had been working on in college, and the kids desperately wanted to learn to play the guitar. I remember talking about this dilemma to the rest of the music staff at one of my first department meetings. One very seasoned teacher was pretty cynical and said, "You will probably have enough money to buy one thing per year, so you'll have everything you need by the time you retire!"

This was not acceptable to me. I thought about my reason for teaching: my *why*. There was not an "if" at the end of my *why* statement. I never said that I wanted to help people discover the music that exists inside of them only *if* my district had enough money to buy instruments! I needed to find a way to get the equipment I needed fast. I asked around, did some digging, and discovered some obvious (and some not so obvious) resources. Within my first three years at the district, I had acquired twenty-five djembes, fifteen more guitars, and have continued to expand the music program and course offerings because of the materials that I have gotten each year for my students.

DONATIONS AND SHARING

I first sent out a district-wide email and posted the need on social media. It's amazing how many instruments sit in closets and attics collecting dust. People are usually very generous and happy to see their old instruments put to good use. It might be a good idea to let your district know your intentions. They could potentially help you with your campaign for instruments through their website and other networks. Consider putting an ad in your local newspaper or, even better, set up an interview for an article.

Other teachers are really our best resources, so reach out to the music teachers in nearby schools. Imagine what we could do if we all helped each other with our ideas to grow our programs. Ask to borrow instruments. This interdependence can lead to many other exciting collaborations across districts.

GRANTS

Over the years I have written a lot of grants. Grant writing is a very effective way to get funding for your program, however, it takes time and careful consideration to make sure the grant aligns with your needs. Look online for a wide range of grants that might be applicable to your program and check in with your local Chamber of Commerce to find out if a local organization or community foundation has a grant program. As you write your grant, be mindful that the language in your application matches the specific requirements.

Once you find an appropriate grant, tell your story! Describe your need and your current situation with the students you teach. Explain why you are requesting funding and the number of students who will be impacted if you are awarded the grant. If your request is simple, concrete, and emotional, the proposal will be more effective.

Answer all of the grant application questions as best as you can. It is easy to overlook something or combine questions that might have a common answer. As you fill out the application, continue to refer back to the mission of the grant and how it relates to your needs. Letters of support are also sometimes necessary. Ask your principal, superintendent, or a school board member for these letters.

Proofread your work and ask lots of people to read your proposal. Your application needs to be accurate and without spelling or grammatical mistakes.

LOCAL BUSINESSES

Reach out to your local music store and explain your plans for instruments or materials. They will be a huge help in guiding you to get the best materials for the best prices. If they don't have something in stock, they can be very resourceful and can point you in the right direction.

Through their business, they generally have lots of connections with many districts and music companies that might be able to help. Sometimes even the local hardware stores can be useful, particularly if you are looking for buckets to use as drums or other materials to make your own classroom instruments.

FUNDRAISING

Before you start a fundraiser, check with your administration about the district or school policy for raising money. Decide what you want to purchase, and much like the grant, be specific when you tell your story. Your students need to understand why they are raising money and when people give money to a fundraiser, they need to know exactly where their money is going. Send out a cover letter with the fundraising materials so everyone understands your classroom needs. Include the long-term effects and the number of students who will benefit. Kids generally enjoy fundraising because they feel a sense of ownership when they help get materials for the school and for their program.

Websites such as Donorschoose.org are another way to fundraise. This website uses crowdsourcing to help teachers access funds for their particular project. The process is very user friendly and there are prompts that guide you through each step. Once the materials have been purchased, students are usually required to send thank you notes which allows them to be a part of the process, have ownership in the program, and show their gratitude to the donors. Occasionally, very generous philanthropists will give up to 50% of your project if you are able to fundraise the other 50%.

GET WHAT YOU NEED

Acquiring materials can sometimes be difficult which is why you need to keep your *why* in the forefront of everything you do. If your *why* is compelling enough, then you will be able to find your way around the obstacles. The *why* is your driving force that will help you persevere through the challenges (like lack of equipment) that may prevent you from doing what you want for your program and your students. It's up to you to make their music experiences inspiring, so go get what you need!

8.
SELF-CARE ISN'T SELFISH

"When we strive to become better than we are,
everything around us becomes better, too."
~ Paulo Coelho, The Alchemist

One of the most important things that ends up getting neglected during the first few years of teaching is YOU. With everything that needs your attention, it's very easy to forget about taking care of yourself. As you continue your teaching career, there will constantly be new things to get used to. Figuring it all out can be exhausting and frustrating. Rest and restoration are essential to sustain your energy, enthusiasm, and focus throughout the year.

What have you done to take care of yourself today? Seriously. Can you answer this? It is not a question that teachers usually ask themselves because we are supposed to take care of everyone else, right? We give so much of ourselves to our job that the personal/professional boundary of self-care seems to get very blurry. Being really busy is something teachers (especially music teachers) tend to wear as a badge of honor. But being busy and feeling run-down are two very different things. And then when we get sick (which is inevitable), everything seems to fall apart!

STAY HEALTHY

Our most prized possession is our health. At school there will be germs. Lots of germs! But, no matter how many times you wash your hands and use the hand sanitizer on your desk, eventually you will get sick. Take the sick day. This is important so I'm going to say it again: Take. The. Sick. Day. There is no need to be a martyr and you are no good to anyone when you are sick. It's necessary to take the time to rest and recover so you can come back to school ready to teach. Your students and coworkers will be fine, and all of the things you need to do can wait. Give yourself permission to take care of yourself first.

Make sure to go the doctor if you need to go. If that means missing school, then that's okay! When I speak with other teachers about being sick, I often hear about all the guilty feelings over missing school. Yes, missing a day can be a huge pain. Sub plans are sometimes a nightmare to prepare if you're lucky enough to even get a sub! But the kids will always be okay. Everyone at work needs you to be healthy so you can be your best for them.

In addition to the sick day, I always advocate for a mental health day. Teaching is tough stuff and it's not for the weak of heart. We give so much of ourselves because our *why* means so much to us. Sometimes it can feel draining. You might not be home coughing or in bed with a stomach bug, but you may need to take a day to get your mind back in the game.

If you feel run-down and start to sense the early symptoms of burnout, take a day for yourself. Do something that makes you feel energized. Don't feel guilty. This is part of self-care. You will be a better teacher when you come back refreshed and refocused. Just as your car can't run without fuel, you can't run on empty either. Fill yourself up with the things that bring you joy. Connect with family, go for a run, take a yoga class, meditate, read a book, play some video games — whatever! Then you can come back the next day ready to get back to your *why*.

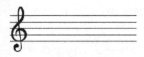

Take a moment and brainstorm some activities that recharge you. Write them down here so you can come back to this list when you need it:

_____

_____

_____

_____

_____

_____

_____

SET BOUNDARIES

Your life will always be changing. Sometimes the things that used to be important to you will move into the background as new priorities take up your time. When I first started teaching, I was fresh out of college and my fiancé (now my husband) and I had to juggle our work schedules with making sure we were home in time for our dog to be walked and fed. Over the years, our jobs changed and work responsibilities shifted. We added a second dog to our family, bought a house and had two children. The choices I make regarding how I spend my time are much different from when it was just my husband, the dog, and me in our little apartment.

When life changed, my priorities changed as well, and I had to learn how to say 'no'. As a new teacher, there can be a lot of pressure to do everything. Most of the time, we feel the need to take on too much, and we eventually pay the price with our physical and mental health. You must realize that there is not enough of you to go around for everyone and everything that may ask for your attention. You can't do everything, and when you feel like you are juggling too many things, nothing can really be done well. We all have a finite amount of time and energy to give, so when you are feeling like you are spread too thin, give yourself permission to say 'no'.

This is about understanding your priorities and setting boundaries, which can be hard as you establish yourself as a new teacher. For the record, this is never easy. You need to find your limits, which might not be possible until you go beyond them, especially at the beginning of your career. If you feel overwhelmed to the point where it becomes paralyzing, take a close look at your responsibilities and figure out if you need to step away from something or respectfully decline something else coming your way. In doing this, you will be able to concentrate your energy on things that really need your full attention (and the things you really want to give your attention to).

To be clear, saying 'no' is not about being selfish. In fact, this is about self-preservation. It's also about doing your job well and creating endurance for longevity in this career. It's very easy to become involved with too many things at school that leave you with very little time and energy for your personal endeavors. You need to be proactive in your choices to avoid burnout. Your boundaries need to be connected to your professional *why* and your personal priorities.

If your boundaries are consistently being crossed, it is possible that your current school or district may not be a good fit. If you experience an overwhelming sense of insecurity, or feel dissatisfied with teaching, it is important to recognize that teaching might not be the problem, but perhaps it can be the school. It might be that the values of the district do not necessarily align with your own. If this is the case, keep an open mind and have the courage to seek out other positions in a district that supports the arts and the work that you do.

BREATHE

As musicians, breathing should be intuitive but, it's not as simple as it seems. In fact, our breath can reflect the way we feel. When we feel stressed and frustrated, our breath gets shallow and rigid. When we are mad, sometimes we hold our breath without even realizing it! Breathing is not just about relaxing, although that is occasionally a happy side effect.

Intentional breathing is about connecting your mind with your body and resetting your brain.

Regain awareness of your breath as often as possible. This can be as simple as taking three to four deep breaths between classes. Your students will be full of energy and come into your classroom with a wide variety of needs. You have to remain stable and steady because the kids are constantly changing, sometimes minute to minute. Mindful breathing will enable you to feel united with your intentions and to stay grounded throughout the day. It's an important self-regulating tool. When you connect with your breath often, you will allow yourself space to be ready for whatever might come your way.

Box breathing is a good restorative breathing technique. Place your tongue behind your top teeth. Breathe in through your mouth for three counts. Hold your breath for three counts. Then exhale for three counts and hold again for three. Take a look at the diagram below:

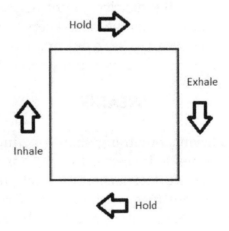

I have actually used box breathing with my students and have been amazed at the results. A rowdy class can become quiet and attentive. An unfocused class can transform immediately into students ready to learn. One time during a general music class, many of my students could not play very simple rhythms in a song which they had played really well in the past. I asked them to put their instruments down and explained the box breathing technique. I guided the breathing exercise for three rounds and then had them pick up their instruments again. I expected them to improve their focus, but didn't anticipate that they would play the song perfectly. I was completely shocked, and now use it as a tool for when my students are feeling extra wiggly.

If it can work well for students, imagine what breathing can do for you throughout your day! It can be helpful to set a timer to remind yourself to breathe. Try it, and notice your breathing when the alarm goes off. Is it shallow or deep? Are you holding your breath? Consider breathing mindfully in tandem with an activity (before lunch, in between classes, when you sit at your desk) so you are more likely to remember to do it and make it a habit.

PERFORMING

We literally perform for a living. We are up in front of some of the hardest audiences every single day: our students! There will be times when you will feel tired. Life happens. Once in a while you will come to work feeling overwhelmed or sad because of something outside of school. It's important to recognize and acknowledge your feelings so you can do something about it. When you are in front of your students, you actually have the ability to influence their mood, which in turn can determine their engagement. Make it count. If you are feeling down, and your energy is low, chances are your students won't be as attentive. You need to perform.

Standing in front of a large group of students is always quite a show. This isn't about entertaining the kids. It's the type of performance that is required so the students want to pay attention and stay engaged for forty minutes. It is about putting the needs of the kids before our own. Sometimes that means putting our own feelings aside so we can focus our attention on our students.

Music teachers already have practice performing. We are in fact trained performers, and often we need to think of our roles as teachers as just that: parts to play. Sometimes we are exhausted, mad, or frustrated. But we must be the teacher the students need us to be every day. To be clear, I am not suggesting that you always hide your emotions from your students. Occasionally it might be helpful and appropriate to tell the students "I'm feeling a little sad today, but we're going to have a great class." Use your professional discretion, and remember to keep your students in mind.

Sometimes when you are feeling a little off, some chocolate might help. Other times, going for a walk around the school building is necessary. Any movement or physical change can actually change your emotional state. Even the simple act of smiling can do the trick (although depending on the situation, sometimes that can be challenging too!) If the weather is good, go outside for a couple of minutes. Just getting some sun on your skin and breathing in the fresh air can turn a 180 on the way you feel.

AND SOME OTHER THINGS TO KEEP IN MIND

• Hydrate! Drink lots of water. You might experience vocal fatigue during the first few weeks until your body builds up the endurance to talk to a large group of kids all day. Rest your voice when you are not at school.

• Use the bathroom! When I surveyed teachers for their advice for a first-year music teacher, this is something that almost everyone mentioned. The very few minutes in between class might be all that you have, but don't wait. Go! Even if that means asking a teacher to hold their class for an extra minute. Your body will thank you!

• Stay organized! You will have a lot of things to keep track of and it can get very overwhelming if you do not have an organizational system in place. Be consistent with entering grades, keeping papers in order, and maintaining important records (inventories, requisitions, permission slips, etc.). Ask for help when you need it. There will be a lot of things you need to do that do not actually involve teaching at all. Staying on top of it all will prevent you from feeling like you're drowning.

• Keep it fresh! Invest in some air freshener because it's incredible how smelly a room can get. Do yourself a favor and keep some Febreeze on hand.

• Be smart about social media! Your school probably has a policy about social media that you need to be aware of, but here are some general guidelines: It is crucial that you maintain healthy boundaries with your personal social media accounts. Don't post pictures of your students on your personal account. While the school may have permission to share photos, you do not. Communication about school events to parents and students should take place on platforms that are endorsed by the school (such as Google Classroom, a school Instagram account, or school Facebook page). You also want to be cautious about what you put on your personal accounts. Don't share information about students, parents, or post negative comments about your school or district. Even if you have your accounts on the highest privacy settings, everything you post can potentially be made public.

• Plan for the future! Set up a retirement fund as soon as you can. Retirement may sound like a lifetime away but the earlier you do this, the better off you will be in the long run. This is one of the many "adulting" things you will do as you begin your career. Your older self will thank you one day.

BE KIND TO YOURSELF

The first few years are hard and it will take some time to find your footing. The anxiety that you might feel about your work means you care about your success and the progress of your students. It's a commendable thought, but be patient and kind to yourself. Anxiety is not helpful especially if it comes from creating unnecessary pressure or setting unreasonable expectations. It's a good idea to keep a folder of good emails and other well wishes and return to it when you are feeling down. It will lift you up and remind you of the joy that pursuing your *why* can bring.

Your thoughts are very powerful, and when things get tough, you may tell yourself that you're not good enough. When you feel insecure, the little voice in the back of your head can get louder, telling you that you are not doing anything right. It can sneak up on you when you are feeling unsure about an observation or you don't feel confident about a lesson because it didn't go as well as you had hoped. The good news is, these are just your thoughts and you are not defined by them. Everyone has bad days. Every teacher has moments when things get too overwhelming. You can choose to stay in a defeated, insecure mindset, or you can tell yourself that it will be OKAY and you have what it takes to be the teacher your students need you to be. Understanding this is hard, and it takes practice, but it can make all the difference.

9.
ON YOUR WAY

"What if I fall?"
"Oh, but my darling, what if you fly?"
~ Erin Hanson

Show yourself respect for where you are now. You are at the beginning of your career. Celebrate that. You have a lifetime ahead full of lessons and learning — for YOU! Give yourself permission to try new things and allow yourself to be comfortable failing. Failing, after all, (as we teach our students), is about learning, getting back up, and trying again. A lesson that completely falls apart is not a reflection on you as a person or a teacher. It's what you do with that failed attempt that will determine who you are as an educator.

LEARN AS YOU GO

You don't know everything. You can't know everything. There is so much beauty in that. Teaching is a long journey of constant learning. Most of the first few years of your career are about trial by fire, but it's what happens afterwards that separates the mediocre teachers from the great ones. Trust yourself that you have good teaching instincts and ask for help when you need it. Remind yourself that you are qualified to do this and if all else fails, fake it 'til you make it! Sometimes it's the false confidence that can get you through a lesson or situation that otherwise makes you feel insecure. At the same time, honor your mistakes. You will definitely mess up and make mistakes. Own them and learn from them. It's the only way you will grow.

Keep this in the back of your mind: try, reflect, adjust, repeat. Reflection can be hard because this means you might actually have to admit you made a mistake or need to take responsibility for something that could have been done better. This may feel uncomfortable, but, do it anyway. When you own your mistakes and missteps, you will learn from them faster. You'll then have the space to try again and improve. When a class doesn't go well, it's so much easier to tell yourself that the students are just a bunch of challenging kids. While that may be the case, you also have a responsibility in that scenario. The band might not play as well as you thought they would. Instead of blaming the lazy students who never practice, what would happen if you got a little more curious about your own teaching and looked for ways to approach the rehearsal differently? Try, reflect, adjust, repeat!

Journaling can be a great tool for reflection. Even just writing a quick paragraph about things that went smoothly and things that didn't work out will be helpful for you. As you keep using the same lesson year after year, you will be able to identify potential pitfalls and address them before they become problematic.

Sometimes a classroom challenge has to do with pacing, a different explanation, or mixing up the order in which the information was presented. Hopefully this book is a good start in this reflection process.

Reflection doesn't always have to be that scary, especially if you train yourself to look for the positive before jumping right into the things that didn't go well. Here is a pretty standard reflection that I use for myself:

1. What went well? Be specific.

2. What was challenging? Why?

3. What can I do differently next time to avoid those challenges?

It's really that simple. You must start with number one. Acknowledge something that was great. Pat yourself on the back for at least one thing that went well, even if it's something small. It's impossible to be receptive to change when you are only focusing on the negative. Be kind to yourself.

ASK FOR HELP

I've said this a lot, but it's worth repeating: ask for help! Don't feel like you need to do everything on your own. There are so many resources that are easily available and literally at your fingertips. Asking a question isn't an admission of helplessness. Asking for help is how we learn. Additionally, when you give other people a chance to help, they will become invested in your success. If you're lucky enough to work in a department with other music teachers in your school, make sure you have a mentor to go to when you get stuck. If you are the only music teacher in your building, find a mentor who teaches music in another school. It might also be a college professor or your student teaching supervisor. Build a community for yourself so you don't feel alone. Go to the state and national music conferences to network with other teachers and join your professional organizations. There are also a ton of great music teachers on social media who share their best practices. We are our own best resources!

FIND THE JOY

Try not to take yourself too seriously. Challenge yourself to be silly, smile often, and laugh. You chose a career where you get to work with kids all day. That's pretty awesome. Be mindful of the beauty and enjoy the moments where you can experience joy; and there will be a lot of joy.

Think back to your *why*. Guide your students to understand the magic they possess when they open their mouths to sing or put an instrument in their hands. In this crazy world we live in, music can help bring us together. Music is what enables people to think outside of the box, experience wonder, and of course, elevate humanity. You've got what it takes to be the teacher you want to be and you now have more tools to help you through the challenges that may come your way. You have the most important job in the world. You are a superhero. You get to change the lives of the children that come through your doors every day. Keep your *why* close, and cherish the music you will make with your students.

10.
ONE FINAL THOUGHT

Since 2009, I have directed an incredible intergenerational choir made up of community members of all ages and musical abilities. The Dryden Area Intergenerational Band and Chorus started in 1996 by an amazing woman, Jody Earle, who wanted to create more musical opportunities for her two sons during the summer months when school was out. This small group kept expanding through the years and has come to be a highlight of the summer for many local residents. There are no auditions; a true come-as-you-are group that rehearses for only six, two-hour rehearsals over the summer with two concerts in August. This choir is magical. I often have two or three generations of families coming to rehearsal to spend their Monday evening singing in an un-air-conditioned church. I have had singers ranging from ages eight to ninety-one, all making music together with a tremendous amount of delight. Their commitment to this group makes me feel incredibly connected to the work that I do during the school year. It is a beautiful example of lifelong music learning.

In 2016, for the 20th anniversary, we had a song commissioned by a local composer to the text of a Henry Cuyler Bunner poem. To me, this poem epitomized how I feel about my purpose as a music teacher. The metaphor of planting seeds graciously paid homage to Jody's vision, who couldn't possibly have known her small idea would have such longevity. As teachers, we too plant seeds, not necessarily seeing or even imagining the results of our influence. We plant seeds with love, hope, and a sense of community knowing one day they will grow.

The Heart of the Tree
By Henry Cuyler Bunner

What does he plant who plants a tree?
He plants a friend of sun and sky;
He plants the flag of breezes free;
The shaft of beauty, towering high;
He plants a home to heaven anigh;
For song and mother-croon of bird
In hushed and happy twilight heard—
The treble of heaven's harmony—
These things he plants who plants a tree.

What does he plant who plants a tree?
He plants cool shade and tender rain,
And seed and bud of days to be,
And years that fade and flush again;
He plants the glory of the plain;
He plants the forest's heritage;
The harvest of a coming age;
The joy that unborn eyes shall see—
These things he plants who plants a tree.

What does he plant who plants a tree?
He plants, in sap and leaf and wood,
    In love of home and loyalty
And far-cast thought of civic good—
His blessings on the neighborhood,
    Who in the hollow of His hand
Holds all the growth of all our land—
    A nation's growth from sea to sea
Stirs in his heart who plants a tree.

HELPFUL RESOURCES

CREATIVITY

It is extremely important to broaden our scope of the idea of creativity. As educators, we sometimes unintentionally take away children's creativity. We are all too often so focused on accuracy that it is easy to lose sight of individual expression and creation in the music classroom. These resources shine a light on how we can foster true creativity in any class.

Big Magic: Creative Living Beyond Fear
by Elizabeth Gilbert

Creative Confidence; Unleashing the Creative Potential Within Us All by David M. Kelley & Tom Kelley

Creativity, Inc. by Ed Catmull and Amy Wallace

Intention; Critical creativity in the classroom
by Amy Burvall & Dan Ryder

Originals: How Non-Conformists Move the World
by Adam Grant

Staying Composed by Dale Trumbore

COMMUNICATION

Good communication is essential for being a successful teacher. These resources will give you some interesting ideas about how to improve your communication skills. This is necessary for talking with our students, parents, colleagues, administrators, and community members.

Crucial Conversations: Tools for Talking When Stakes are High by Kerry Patterson, Joseph Grenny, Ron McMillan, & Al Switzler

Give and Take: A Revolutionary Approach to Success by Adam Grant

If I Understood You, Would I Have this Look on my Face? by Alan Alda

Thanks for the Feedback: The Science and Art of Receiving Feedback Well by Douglass Stone & Sheila Heen

SCHOOL CULTURE

You can achieve monumental change in your school by creating a safe, welcoming space for students and staff. Sometimes these efforts will spread to the greater school community. Consider how music can be a vehicle for culture change at school.

All Kids are our Kids: What Communities Must Do to Raise Caring and Responsible Children and Adolescents by Peter L. Benson

Empathy: Why it Matters and How to Get It
by Roman Krznaric

*Go Together: How the Concept of Ubuntu Will Change
the Way You Live, Work, and Lead* by Shola Richards

Grit: The Power of Passion and Perseverance
by Angela Duckworth

Mindset: The New Psychology of Success
by Carol S. Dweck

*Teaching Children to Care: Management in the
Responsive Classroom by* Ruth Charney

*Unselfie: Why Empathetic Kids Succeed in our
All-About-Me World* by Michele Borba

ADVOCACY

Marketing books are extremely helpful in learning strategies to advocate for music programs. Marketing is not just about products. It's about sharing ideas and having others embrace them. We want our community, administrators, and students to understand and remember the importance of their music education. There is a huge overlap between education and marketing.

Made to Stick: Why Some Ideas Survive and Others Die
by Chip Heath & Dan Heath

*The Tipping Point: How Little Things Can Make a
Big Difference* by Malcolm Gladwell

*This is Marketing: You Can't Be Seen Until You Learn
to See* by Seth Godin

*To Sell is Human: The Surprising Truth About Moving
Others* by Daniel H. Pink

CLASSROOM MANAGEMENT/ CHILD DEVELOPMENT

Classroom management is really about knowing your students. Their developmental needs should inform your lessons and teaching strategies. When you become an expert in the age level that you teach, your classroom will be a place where your students can thrive. Understanding your student's brain development can help in planning your lessons.

Brainstorm: The Power and Purpose of the Teenage Brain by Daniel J. Seigel

No Drama Discipline: The Whole-Brain Way to Calm the Chaos and Nurture Your Child's Developing Mind by Daniel J. Siegel & Tina Payne Bryson

Responsive Classroom for Special Areas, Center for Responsive Schools, Inc.

Self-Reg: How to Help Your Child (and You) Break the Stress Cycle and Successfully Engage with Life by Stuart Shanker

The Whole Brain Child: 12 Revolutionary Strategies to Nurture Your Child's Developing Mind by Dan Siegel & Tina Payne Bryson

This We Believe: Keys to Educating Young Adolescents, National Middle School Association, Association for Middle Level Education

PERSONAL AND PROFESSIONAL GROWTH

As educators, we need to constantly be learners and grow in our field. We also need to take care of ourselves. Keep yourself inspired and find joy in your life outside of school so you can share it with your students when you are in school.

168 Hours: You Have More Time Than You Think by Laura Vanderkam

Dare to Lead: Brave Work, Tough Conversations, Whole Hearts by Brene Brown

Happy Teachers Change the World: A Guide for Cultivating Mindfulness in Education by Thich Nhat Hanh & Katherine Weare

Seven Habits of Highly Effective People: Powerful Lessons in Personal Change by Stephen R. Covey

The Book of Joy: Lasting Happiness in a Changing World by Dahli Lama, Desmond Tutu, et al.

Worthy Human: Because You are the Problem and the Solution by Tracy Litt

ACKNOWLEDGEMENTS

This book would not be possible without the help of some incredible people. Thank you first to my husband, Kevin, and my two amazing children, who have been extremely patient and supportive throughout this process.

A huge thanks to my sister, Rachel who has always been my coach, soundboard, and cheerleader in all of my endeavors. Your guidance with this project has been tremendous in helping me realize my vision.

For my awesome friends, family, and colleagues who happily read all of my drafts, thank you for asking questions and giving me valuable feedback. You challenged me to look deeper into my writing. Thank you Molly Andrejko for your unending support and creative ideas. And thank you Rebecca Fagen Houghton for being a lifelong friend. I am so glad that this project gave us a reason to connect more frequently.

To all of my teachers and mentors throughout the years, I am grateful for your lessons. You have encouraged me to always seek knowledge for better understanding, and empowered me to share it with others. Thank you especially to Eric Williams, Walter Lastowski, Verna Brummett, Deborah Montgomery-Cove, Jennifer Aylmer, and Keith Kaiser.

And of course, thank YOU! You read this book because you strive to be better at your craft. You show up for your students every day and do an outstanding job. Thank you for your efforts and dedication to this profession. You are making the world a better place.

ABOUT THE AUTHOR

Jen has spent her career in Central New York teaching students of all ages. She has a Bachelor's degree in music education and vocal performance, and a Master's degree in music education from Ithaca College. She frequently writes articles for the Alfred Music blog, and has been published in *School Music News*, the New York State School Music Association's monthly publication, and *In Transition*, the publication for the New York State Middle School Association. Her commitment to education has taken her to a national platform as a guest conductor for elementary and middle school choirs, and as a clinician for music education conferences. She has very fond memories of joy, frustration, tears, and inspiration during her first few years of teaching, and wouldn't trade them for anything.

Jenrafferty.com
Facebook.com/JenRaffertyMusic
Instagram: @Jenraffertymusic